Surviving Paranoid Schizophrenia:

A Real Life Story

D1477796

John Brown M.A

chipmunkapublishing
the mental health publisher

H46 683 247 7

Published by
Chipmunkapublishing
PO Box 6872
Brentwood
Essex CM13 1ZT
United Kingdom

http://www.chipmunkapublishing.com

ISBN   978-1-84991-960-9

Chipmunkapublishing   gratefully   acknowledge   the support of Arts Council England.

Contents

About the Author

The author would like to issue this statement to all readers:

"I make statements about Allah, Islam, the prophet Muhammad, the Koran and Muslims (May peace be upon them) in this book, solely in the course of describing my symptoms and delusions of paranoid schizophrenia, which is my mental illness. In no way do I wish to insult or cause any offense, harm, hurt or denigration to Allah, Islam, the prophet Muhammad, the Koran or Muslims and I wish that peace be upon them all. I do sincerely apologize to all my honorable Muslim readers in advance for any unintended insult, harm, hurt or offense caused, and sincerely wish them to know that this is neither my intention nor the intention of my book. This is not an anti-Islam book. This book is my real life story about surviving paranoid schizophrenia, a severe and chronic mental illness. It is my hope that this book will inform and educate the general public, social workers, doctors, psychiatrists, psychologists, carers and the academic community about paranoid schizophrenia. I also hope that this book will assist sufferers of paranoid schizophrenia to survive it" (John Brown 2012).

John Brown was born in 1968 in London, England. He left school in Holland Park, London at the age of 16 with GCSEs in English, Science and History. He worked in the construction industry in London to save up enough money to travel to Bangkok, Thailand, where he ended up getting married and teaching English for 7 years. With his teaching experience and jobs he was accepted onto a British university M.Ed course in 1995, from which he graduated with a post graduate diploma in Education in 1998. He taught at schools in Istanbul, Turkey from 1999 – 2000, where he started a university M.A degree course in teaching English, from which he graduated with his M.A degree in 2004. He obtained his CELTA certificate from the University of Cambridge in 2006 in London and his DELTA certificate in 2009 also from the University of Cambridge, while he was teaching in Hong Kong. John Brown is a fully qualified English teacher. He had 2 spells teaching in Indonesia, from 1992 - 1994 with the English Education Centre in Jakarta, and from 2003 – 2004 again in Indonesia, for English First. John also taught at colleges in London from 2000 – 2003, and during 2006. John taught in Hong Kong from 2007 – 2010. Altogether, John has been teaching for 21 years, since starting in Bangkok as a native-speaker in 1989. John was diagnosed with paranoid schizophrenia by psychiatrists in a psychiatric hospital in London after his third psychotic, schizophrenic episode in London in 2005, at the age of 36. John now takes his medication religiously, and very seriously every day to stay mentally well, and to live a good life. He has 1 daughter who is 21, studying for a B.A degree in politics at university in the U.K. John Brown has now settled down into being a life long atheist.

The Background

I've got paranoid schizophrenia; I'm a paranoid schizophrenic. Paranoid schizophrenia has been defined as: a slowly progressive deterioration of the personality, involving withdrawal from reality, social apathy, emotional instability, delusions and hallucinations. The exact cause of my paranoid schizophrenia at the age of 30 in 1998 could be genetic or environmental or a mixture of both. My grandmother on my mother's side, Anna Brown, was extremely delusional in a grandiose way. She used to be deluded that she was descended from a royal, German family and that, therefore, she was really an aristocratic, German princess and not the common, poverty stricken, German, refugee housewife of my Swiss, refugee grandfather's, which the harsh reality of real life and the real world positioned her to be. My schizophrenia, then, could have been genetically inherited from her, although her own mental health was never formally assessed.

Alternatively, it could have been genetically inherited from my Rumanian, refugee grandfather 'Pop' on my father's side. He definitely had some form of schizophrenia, as he was given electric shock treatment for it in a mental hospital in the 1960s, in the old days before my time, when they hadn't yet developed the highly effective anti psychotic medication for it, as they have nowadays. Eventually, he ended his own life in the 1960s by turning on the gas for the gas oven and sticking his head into the oven to commit suicide by gassing himself to death. So both Anna and Pop, or either, could have passed the mental illness onto me through shared, hereditary genes. It's still something of an unsolved puzzle for me.

The other possibility, as a contributory social factor, is that my own mother and the rather dire circumstances of my upbringing as a child unbalanced my brain enough to cause my paranoid schizophrenia at the age of 30. My mum was a radical, feminist fanatic, who, in my opinion, hated men. She was an accountant and graduated from school with 'A' levels as a teenager. She was always going on to me about what bastards they were and I was one of them. She hated my father after their divorce in the late sixties for trying to get custody of me and my sister, which he failed to do. And she poisoned my mind against him and brainwashed me into hating him too, throughout my childhood. This had an extremely negative effect on me as I was going to be a man when I grew up. She then generalized her hatred of him to all men by becoming a feminist fanatic, which was manifested by her giving lengthy, monologue speeches at home to anyone who would listen to her, about what bastards men were for oppressing women. As a consequence, I was then forced to suppress whatever male identity I had, in order to survive in the same house as her for my entire childhood and my teenage years, and so that she didn't persecute me. In this way, she was inadvertently brainwashing me to hate myself as a man and it was this self-hatred that I grew up with. In this way, self-hatred became a mental and emotional ingredient of my personality. She tried to do her best for me, encouraging me when I played for my school and scouts' football teams, and taking me to division 1 football matches every weekend.

I didn't know my dad very well because I grew up only seeing him on weekends throughout my childhood. He taught me to fish and often took me on day long fishing trips at weekends. He also took me for long walks in the country and, at the age of 12, took me to shoot his rifles on registered firing ranges in the countryside. I wasn't allowed to eat sweets or watch television when I visited him and he refused to give me any pocket money at all too. He was a pilot, very interested in machines and he often took me on rides on his motorbike. He was very strict and I didn't really enjoy going to see him when I was a teenager because it was so boring with him. He gave me an ultimatum when I was 13, in which he basically said that I had to decide whether I wanted to see him every weekend or not and when I said I didn't, that was the end. I actually preferred to go to football matches with my mum on Saturdays or to go out with my teenage friends around London, because I was more interested in spending time with girls at weekends, than seeing my dad. He never understood that. It was his father who had been admitted to a mental hospital with schizophrenia in his lifetime and who had ended up killing himself when my father was still a child. Perhaps my dad had mental health problems too.

Then there was the abundant marijuana at home, which was openly available to all the white, hippie and violent, black, boyfriend visitors to my mother's flat throughout the 1970s and 1980s, when I was growing up, developing and delicately trying to develop my own personality and intellect. I was born in 1968 and my mother was heavily into the peace, love, marijuana and socialism of the hippie scene, especially the marijuana. Of course, by the time I was 5 years old I was used to it being smoked all the time in the flat by all visitors and by the time I was 14, I was actively searching the house whenever mum was out, to steal it and smoke it myself. All of my best friends at school were into smoking marijuana too, so we all used to meet up regularly to smoke it together. Between the ages of 14 and 17 then, I was smoking it every day and unbalancing my still young and developing brain with it before the psychiatric term of 'Cannabis Psychosis' had been coined publicly by the psychiatric community. This was the other possible cause – my environment, including my mother and all her marijuana at my young age.

However, I continued to use marijuana regularly and independently until 1998, when I was 30, so there was possibly more than enough paranoia in my brain from it and an imbalance of chemicals caused by it too, to cause the permanent onset of my current paranoid schizophrenia. At one point in my teens, I was smoking 10 joints a day of the best hashish and marijuana in London. The day when I smoked a marijuana reefer at 8 o'clock in the morning, before going to my secondary school classes is still a blur. Now, at 42 years of age, instead of a 10 pound draw of marijuana, I am, and will be, taking 20 milligrams of olanzapine anti-psychotic medication a day for the rest of my life to keep my schizophrenia at bay. Needless to say, I failed at almost everything at secondary school because my mind was usually in a haze of marijuana throughout all my teenage school years. I simply wasn't interested in school anyway. Finally, I left school in 1984 at 16, unskilled, uneducated, unqualified and ignorant, and signed straight onto the dole to get unemployment benefit every fortnight. I had passed GCSE exams in English, Science and History but good jobs and careers required 'A' level examinations for school leavers, which I didn't have.

My first job to get off the dole when I was 17 was as a tea boy and building site laborer on a local building site in Holland Park, London. The pay was just about 50 pounds a week after tax. That job only lasted a month before I was so abused, exploited and exhausted I couldn't suffer it anymore. Then I got a job as a clean laundry deliverer with a laundry company in London, which lasted longer, for approximately 7 months. This was followed by a month at McDonalds and a month at Kentucky Fried Chicken before I got a better paying job on a building site – this time as a well-paid laborer for 150 pounds a week. By this time, however, I was 19 and my mum and her latest boyfriend had had enough of me being a bum and bumming around at home in clouds of marijuana smoke, so they financed me with 2000 pounds in November 1987 to go and visit Thailand and travel and train in Thai boxing there, which I'd taken up initially in London when I was 17. That was my latest interest, which had turned me into an extremely violent person. I usually spent on average 10 to 20 hours a week practicing Thai boxing in my spare time and my life was all terribly self-destructive.

So I went off to Thailand to travel for 6 months, and realized while I was there that I was neither good or skillful enough, or violent enough to be a professional Thai boxer, as I'd originally planned. Nevertheless, having a hard man, tough guy image still appealed to me, probably because I wasn't good enough at anything else, apart from football, which hadn't worked out for me either. So I didn't have any positive or constructive things to focus on in my life to move my life forward in any ways at all. Football hadn't worked out for me because I had turned down an offer to leave home and train with Southend at 16, preferring instead to retreat into my marijuana and reggae world in my room at my mum's in London. I continued to smoke Marijuana in abundance on my trip to Thailand. It was very strong stuff there, possibly the best in the world. I travelled to the islands of Koh Samet, Koh Samui and Koh Phangan, where there were always good and strong supplies of Marijuana for tourists. I would sit outside my bungalows on the beaches for days and nights and smoke it as much as possible. Occasionally, I would spend periods of time swimming in the beautiful sea there but mostly I got stoned out of my mind continually. I made my 2000 pounds last for 6 months by being a backpacker and living the cheap, hippie, backpacking lifestyle. I stayed in the cheapest places, ate the cheapest food and economized wherever I could on expenses.

On returning to my mother's house in London in May 1988 from my travels at 20, I quickly realized I had to get a job and move out, which I did because I got a job as a building site laborer again, and rented a room independently on Holland Road in west London, where I learned to live alone. Initially, I got a job as a laborer working on a nice street in the Holland Park Avenue area, where a house was being done up. I worked on a second laboring job of doing the Mangrove cafe up on All Saints Road, where I had previously gone years before to buy Marijuana from the street dealers there. All Saints Road was previously known as the 'frontline' to locals like me because it was a place where one could go any time of the day or night to buy Marijuana from any of the abundant street dealers there. That was in the days before the police closed the entire street down and arrested all the dealers there in the 1980s. The only other place to go in London at that time was the famous Railton Road in Brixton, where there were also abundant street dealers of Marijuana hanging out around the clock to sell their wares. However, the police also managed to close all of that down too in the 1980s. At the Mangrove building site on All Saints Road, I searched the whole place to try and find any stashes of Marijuana that might have been hidden there, without success. My third laboring job was just off Fleet Street in central London in 1989. And it was at this job where I finally managed to save up my financial target of 2000 pounds and the price of a single ticket back to Bangkok, where I planned to get jobs teaching English and travel some more, while living as cheaply as I could for as long as I could, to escape from my life of drudgery in London. This would enable me to leave my filthy life of London building sites behind.

In June 1989 at the age of 21, I returned to Bangkok and started teaching English immediately, as an unqualified native-speaker for one of the many unprofessional, cowboy language schools that operated in Bangkok at that time. I had absolutely no qualifications, teaching knowledge or skills at that stage. I simply used to turn up at private students' houses and speak English to them for 2 hours a session, two or three times a week, per student. However, my employer, a Thai-Chinese businessman, convinced me that I was teaching 'speaking', and so I was able to convince myself that I really was, and could be, a 'teacher'. I earned 50 pounds a week, which was enough to live cheaply on at that time. I rented a small guest house room for 1 pound a night and spent 2 pounds a day on cheap street food on Khao San Road. I soon realized that this was all I wanted to do with my life – live in Thailand, teach English and marry a beautiful Thai woman. I decided to try and find a nice, straight, decent, honest, Thai woman to settle down with at the age of 22. I also took to Theravada Buddhism in Thailand and became a convert. I would sometimes go to some of the many Buddhist temples in Bangkok to pray and meditate. I bought some Buddha images for myself and hung them around my neck to protect me from evil and to encourage good Karma for myself.

I met my future wife, whose name was 'Dam'- meaning black in Thai, because she had dark skin - at a laundry shop off Khao San Road in Bangkok, where I used to take my weekly laundry to be cheaply cleaned. She was the same age as me - 21. She was a poor, southern Thai, fishing village girl from the southern province of Prachuap Khiri Khan. She worked at the laundry to send money to her poor family in the south. She had to leave school in the south at the age of 14 she said because she had to support herself and her younger brother and sister, which her family couldn't afford to do. That was the reason why she had come to Bangkok to work. As we were both ignorant, uneducated, working class and poor, we got on quite well together because we had those characteristics in common. Typically, I would drop my laundry off and spend time chatting her up in the hope that she would be my first nice, clean, decent, straight girlfriend. I had had a previous Thai 'girlfriend', who I had met in a guesthouse I was staying in just off Khao San Road in July 1989, just after I arrived there. She knocked on my door and brought me a bag of Marijuana, which I thought was perfect, then we made love in my room. Her name was 'Em'. She was 24 and she was a poor girl from the north of Thailand from a place called Khaempeng Phet. We slept together numerous times and I had fallen deeply in love with her, until I found out that she 'worked' nights at bars in Soi Cowboy, which was a well known men's 'entertainment' centre in Bangkok. This was the major reason that we broke up in August 1989 and I decided to focus on my pretty, laundry shop girlfriend Dam, instead. I started to take Dam out to the cinema every week, and to high class restaurants to eat. Slowly, we became boyfriend and girlfriend and I was happy with her because she had a straight job, and was pretty. When we slept together for the first time after 6 months of going out together, she insisted that we had to get married, so I made my promise of marriage to her. Once we started sleeping together, it wasn't long before she became pregnant, so we got married at a registry office in Banglamphu, Bangkok and my daughter was born in Bangkok in June 1991 at the Seventh Day Adventist hospital. Mostly, I was busy teaching English all the time at various locations throughout Bangkok. Some days, I would have to take 10 buses back and forth to various students' addresses in Bangkok to teach. There were classes from 10 am to 12 pm, 2pm to 4 pm and 6 pm to 8 pm, so I was extremely busy working and saving money for myself and my new family.

Once my daughter had arrived, I thought it better to return to London for a visit and to try and look for another job outside of Thailand because we had been the subject of some Thai racism from the general public there, who were very condescending to us because we were a mixed marriage couple and my daughter was Eurasian. Polite, 'educated', Thai society seemed to wrongly assume at that time that any Thai woman with a foreign man was a prostitute, which definitely wasn't true of my wife, who was actually just a hard working, village girl. Anyway, many Thais were intolerant of mixed couples like us because they were racist. In addition, when we went out together and people saw that I was a foreigner, the prices of goods we wanted to buy would suddenly increase 2 or 3 fold. So we moved to London for 6 months to stay with my mother at her house. I had had enough of Thailand at the time and thought it would be better to try to find another job somewhere else in Asia. Then in May 1992 while looking for a new job in London, I managed to get another English teaching job in Jakarta, Indonesia, which had been advertised in a newspaper, so we moved there to live from May.

Indonesia was an interesting place to live at that time. It is geographically a very beautiful country. President Soeharto was in power as he had been since the late 1960s, when he took control after President Sukarno's reign. The poverty of most of the people seemed to be extreme to us and there were gangs of unemployed, impoverished youths roaming the streets or just hanging out with nothing to do, who looked as if they were on the verge of committing violent crimes to feed themselves. Indeed, I was out walking around one day in Jakarta in 1993, when I was confronted by a violent group of young men who demanded money. When I started to run away from them, they chased me and tried to kick and push me over to mug me and/or beat me up, but luckily for me I was able to just keep on running until I was far enough away from them to then hide on a busy main street, where there were lots of people.

My wife, daughter and I had a nice house in Jakarta, which was about 5 minutes walk from my school, so we lived a comfortable middle class life there. However, we still weren't happy. When our Indonesian neighbors found out that my wife was Thai and couldn't speak Indonesian, they took a disliking to us because she wasn't really one of them. After the traditional, Indonesian prayers one Friday, the neighbors stood in front of our house and threw mud at our front door, which stuck to the door. I had to open it later to scrape the mud off. That was just one of the insults we suffered as a mixed race couple in Indonesia. There were good times too. We went to beautiful beaches with friends around Java and visited the beautiful mountains in Puncak outside Jakarta. I often took my daughter swimming when I wasn't working at school to a 5 star hotel swimming pool in central Jakarta.

While I was teaching in Jakarta for 2 years, I met 2 Americans who befriended me and persuaded me to go back to Thailand and work for them in their new international school that they were setting up, in the northern Thai city of Chiang Mai. One of them was Bruce. Bruce was a Californian whose Indonesian neighbors had knocked at his door at his house in Jakarta and threatened to burn him, his Indonesian girlfriend and his house down, if he ever brought her back to his house again, because it was against Islam for her to visit him in his house. I agreed with Bruce that this was absolutely crazy and that he should come to stay with me and my family at my house for a while, because we lived in a different area of Jakarta that I thought was safer than his. Together, we quietly agreed that Indonesia wasn't a good place to live as we felt scared after the experiences that had happened to us at the hands of our Indonesian neighbors. My wife was also adamant that she wanted us to leave Indonesia when my 2 year teaching contract came to an end. Thus, my decision was made to move back to Thailand to the northern city of Chiang Mai with Bruce and another American friend and to teach there at their new international school in 1994, after 2 years in Jakarta.

When we arrived back in Thailand in May 1994, I decided to buy the Koran in Bangkok to try to understand just what the Indonesian Muslims believed. I felt that maybe it was my fault that my experiences in Indonesia had been mostly negative because I hadn't tried to understand the Indonesian people and their culture well enough. This was the first time for me to read any religious literature at all. My family had never been religious at all. None of us had ever gone regularly to church or believed in the Christian faith. Apart from the occasional cub - scout visits to church as a boy or references to God in the national anthem, I had never given it a second thought. I definitely didn't believe in God, although I was still a nominal Buddhist, after converting during my previous visit to Thailand. After a 2 week visit to Bangkok, my wife, daughter and I went up to Chiang Mai in the north, so that I could start teaching in my new school. My wife found a lovely, spacious, 2 bedroom house with a garden for us to rent and we moved in straightaway. My family seemed to be happy at last. My wife was back in her own country and free to go anywhere she pleased, after living with the limitations of Jakarta for 2 years. I read the Koran enthusiastically from start to finish but didn't find anything in it that I thought was believable or in the slightest interest to me. I started teaching at school and my job was going well. My daughter started pre-kindergarten classes at the school at the age of 3 and she was growing up nicely and making good progress. Around this time at school, I met Katherine, who was the mother of one of the kids at my school. She persuaded me to visit her at her house for one of her astrology readings because she was a spiritualist. She gave me a detailed astrology reading of my life and converted me into being interested in spiritualism. From her, I started to believe that I somehow had to search for the mysterious 'light' in my life.

When I made friends with the other teachers at the school and they found out that I had been living in Indonesia, one of them decided to give me the Bible to read. I started to study the Bible in my spare time and to believe in it. I thought I had found the mysterious 'light' that had been missing from my life. Then I managed to persuade my wife that we should become Christians. A week or so after that, walking around in Chiang Mai one Saturday, I met a man called Mark. After talking to him for a while it transpired that he was an American missionary pastor, and had just recently moved to Chiang Mai with his wife and kids on a mission for God from his Lutheran church in America, Texas to be exact. I asked him if he would be prepared to give me Bible study classes every Saturday afternoon for 2 hours and he said that he would. From then on, I attended his Bible study classes at his house for the next few months. Things seemed to be going well with my new found Christian faith, so I then persuaded my wife that we should attend his Lutheran church services every Sunday morning at his house.

It wasn't long before both my wife and I had become quite devout Christians and Mark baptized us both into the faith with a formal baptism ceremony straight from the Bible at his house. Mark, his wife Shelley and their 2 kids and my wife, daughter and I then developed a very friendly relationship in which we would regularly visit each other, go out for walks around Chiang Mai and go out to eat at restaurants together. I soon became absolutely convinced that my trip to Indonesia had been a kind of spiritual and religious wake-up call from God directly to me, in order to make me become a Christian. I felt that the Bible and Christianity had filled a huge void in my life. At the same time, I was studying for an M.Ed degree with a British university and I had to make occasional trips to Singapore to attend study schools there. My life seemed to be going well and my family and I were settling down in Chiang Mai, and were extremely happy. My daughter was enjoying school and making friends there, which made her very happy. I organized and trained a school football team, which played against some other schools in Chiang Mai with some success, so my students really took a liking to me and this made me a very popular teacher with them. However, once I had got my first essay assignment done for my university in December 1995, I decided that I should leave Chiang Mai and change schools, as I didn't get on very well with the principal of my school any more. I had become unhappy and dissatisfied with my job and decided a change was needed in my life.

I told my wife that we should move down south to Pattaya, where God would help us and where I could look for another job. Mark wasn't pleased and didn't want us to go but I was convinced that I could have a better life elsewhere. That was me – sometimes doing unusual things and making big decisions on a whim. My wife found us a big, comfortable house to live in, in Pattaya and I got a teaching job with the international school of Pattaya in March 1996. Then my daughter went to school there and started studying in year 1. We used to go to school together every morning after a quick breakfast that my wife would prepare. Still Christians, we attended the local international church every Sunday and made new friends there. Then I was asked by the resident pastor to give sermons every

Sunday at the church, which I enthusiastically agreed to do. I gave 2 or 3 sermons at the church before the end of my school term in June 1996, which I enjoyed. Then one of my congregation offered to financially support me to be trained at a Christian Bible college. I was seriously considering his offer while I was looking for other jobs for the new school term starting in September 1996. Then the first thing that happened was that I got a job to teach at an international school in Korat, in north-eastern Thailand from August 1996. Luxury accommodation was included in the teaching contract and we travelled up to the school with all our belongings on a pick-up truck. My wife was very pleased with the new housing in Korat and we quickly settled in with my daughter starting school in September. The accommodation was a fully furnished 2 bedroom bungalow with modern appliances.

My new job was great. I had finished my second essay assignment in Pattaya and now I was on my third, which I got down to straight away and as quickly as I could. At that point, I knew I didn't have the time anymore to study to be a Pastor at a Christian college, so I dropped the idea. My teaching and my essay were going well at my new school and my daughter was learning a lot in her new year 1 class. I felt I was very successful then with the best job I'd had so far and a luxury bungalow to live in. I soon finished my third essay assignment for university and sent it off. The news soon came back that I'd passed. However, a new principal came to the school and decided he didn't want any of the current staff to be his teachers, so we all, me included, had to move on for no particular reason. This was in December 1996. A group of teachers filed court cases against the school for breaches of their contracts but I didn't bother. I moved my family back down to Pattaya in January 1997, rented a house there and went to look for a new school yet again.

I had saved up a lot of money from my job in Korat, so we lived well in Pattaya until I found a new school in August 1997 in Bangkok. We moved into an apartment in Bangkok in August, my daughter started school with me to complete her grade 1 studies and I had my own grade 2 class to teach. I finished my fourth essay assignment in Pattaya and it was a pass, so now I was on my final 20,000 word dissertation for my British M.Ed degree. I was working hard on my teaching in class with my kids every day from 8am to 4.30 pm and I was writing my dissertation every day including weekends in all my spare time. The months went by and my dissertation was going well. However, I was extremely exhausted by it all and I needed lots of rest and sleep because of all the stress I was under – working hard and writing my dissertation. Then one day when I thought I had finished my dissertation, I sent it off to my university.

A few days after that, I started to receive what I thought were psychic, supernatural messages from God, through God's holy spirit. I suddenly came to believe that God wanted me to divorce my wife and have a love affair with a Filipino teacher, who I was working with at school. I felt I was supposed to meet this Filipino woman and start an affair with her, so that is what I decided to do because of my supernatural messages from God. I called her and she agreed to meet me. Her name was Sue and we started going out together in Bangkok. We went to restaurants and clubs together for about a month but when I told her of my feelings for her, she refused to get involved. I made my wife move out of our apartment because I wanted to be alone with Sue due to the delusions I was having about receiving messages from God. The whole situation just ended up in chaos. I knew my marriage was over because I had fallen in love with Sue. Sue was 38 and she was married to her

Filipino husband. They had 4 children together in the Philippines and this is who God was telling me to have an affair with. Perhaps that was the first real sign of my impending mental illness.

I decided to divorce my Thai wife. I had had enough of married life and didn't feel young, free and independent any more. My wife's nagging, moaning and complaining about money and everything else was driving me mad and although I loved my daughter tremendously, and wanted her to grow up with me, I felt I couldn't stay with my wife just for the sake of my daughter. My principal at my school in Bangkok found out that I was having an affair with Sue, so he fired me from my teaching job at the school. Realizing that my wife would get custody of our daughter, if we got divorced, I took my daughter away to live with me in a remote Thai border village neighboring Burma. It wasn't long before my wife and my mother turned up with the Thai police, took my daughter away with them, and forbade me to follow. The next thing I knew was that my wife and my daughter were in London with my mother and my wife was applying for custody through the courts. I knew then that I had to return to London too to see my daughter, so I got the next available flight that I could. Once I got back to London in August 1998, I got a job delivering laundry in Hammersmith hospital and rented a small single room off Shepherd's Bush Road in Sulgrave Road, so I could be available to visit my daughter. However, I wasn't allowed by my wife or mother to see my daughter – I wasn't given any access to her at all. And I found out that my wife had successfully got custody of my daughter through the courts in October 1998.

My daughter was only 7 years old at that time. Up to that point I had done almost everything I could with her, to bring her up and take care of her. I had got her into all of the English speaking international schools, where I had worked in Thailand. I had done all of her homework with her and read her bedtime stories every night from all of the children's books I had bought for her. I had got her nice food that I knew she enjoyed from shops and restaurants. I had taught her to read and write by the age of 5. I had taught her to swim and got her first bicycle for her and taught her to ride it. We had always been on holidays together and had great times together. I had bought her a whole collection of Disney cartoon videos, which she loved and we often used to watch them together. Her particular favorites were the Lion King, Peter Pan, the Fox and the Hound and the Little Mermaid. She also used to spend weekends watching them by herself. I had also filled her bedroom with beautiful teddy bears and other cuddly toys, which she loved. My daughter seemed to be happy and she was enjoying herself at school and with her friends there. We had always been very close and now my wife had decided that it was all over between my daughter and I. My wife had selfishly decided that my daughter didn't need me anymore, that she only needed her mother and that she would bring her up as a one parent family. I felt that my wife was exacting revenge on me for having a love affair with Sue. But 'what could I do?', I asked myself. I thought that was what God had told me to do.

The First Signs of Schizophrenia?

My wife getting custody of my daughter, my daughter now permanently residing with my wife and me not having access to her, completely destroyed me emotionally and mentally. In addition, I had lost my job at my school in Bangkok because I had had an affair with Sue and I found out that my dissertation was a fail because I hadn't carried out my university professor's instructions to re-write parts of it that were unsatisfactory. I was only to receive a post graduate diploma in Education and not the full M.Ed degree that I'd expected to get after all. My whole life seemed to have just fallen apart on all fronts: job, marriage, educational career and my fatherhood relationship with my daughter. I sat in my little rented room and became more and more depressed as the months went by, without seeing my daughter and without having graduated from university with a full Master's degree. It was all extremely depressing for me. I'd spent months alone in my room continually traumatizing, thinking, missing and worrying about my daughter. I would stare at the walls for hours on end full of tears, sadness and depression. I spent hours on end sobbing about her.

Finally, the mental pressure of all the months of trauma suddenly snapped and ripped something inside my brain, which I distinctly felt. I was kneeling on the floor of my room praying with my Bible open on the floor and my head resting on it, face down. I was also holding a knife to my own throat, on the brink of suicide, with a tremendous throbbing pain of sadness in my head, when suddenly I felt a huge rip inside my brain and a voice saying 'I hate you Jesus' and I saw 2 angels descending from heaven and pulling my soul out of my body through my head, which was exploding with pain. They then carried my soul with them up to heaven, which I saw outside my window, and then I saw that my soul had entered heaven with them. Amazingly, I found that I could look up and see heaven in a spiritual way for the first time in my life.

By now, it was the end of 1998 and I hadn't seen my daughter for about 4 months. I was sure I was going to have a heart attack and die from all the pain, stress, depression, sadness and mental and emotional trauma that I was going through. I was going through a complete mental and emotional breakdown and cracking up completely. I believed that God had taken pity on the suffering of my spirit, and had sent angels down to collect it and take it to heaven. I then began regularly to see and hear angels talking to me from heaven. I also started to believe that I was really Jesus Christ in the second coming as described in the book of Revelation in the Bible because of all the spiritual voices that I could hear that I imagined were coming from heaven directly to me. I imagined that I was receiving messages from God directly from heaven.

As time passed and my mental state deteriorated even further, I began to see frightening looking demons coming into my room by walking through the solid wooden door and the solid walls to enter and haunt, possess and terrorize me. I also saw Satan the Devil appear to me in the hallway outside my room, where he tried to speak to me, but I ran away without listening to him because I was so terrified of what I was seeing and hearing. I was living a nightmare of paranoid schizophrenic delusions that evil was haunting and persecuting me and that I might be possessed by the Devil or his evil spirits at any time of the day or night. I knew it was Satan because he had the most evil eyes I had ever seen, he was transparent and he had wings on his back, horns on his head and an arrow pointed tail. He also told me that his name was 'Lucifer', which was one of the names of the Devil from the Bible. Now that I could see and hear all manner of spirits, angels and demons in my room, I began to believe that I was chosen by God to hear messages from heaven and hell. I believed I was psychic, and had some sort of special, spiritual calling to hear, see and receive messages directly from God and other supernatural phenomena. I believed I was especially chosen to be on some secret, special, supernatural, mystical mission in life from God. However, I also believed that the evil spirits and demons were sent by Satan to persecute me and to try to gain possession of my body and mind. No other explanation for what I was seeing, hearing and being haunted by in my room seemed possible.

These were, arguably, my first paranoid, persecutory delusions of schizophrenia. I was hearing voices and seeing visions that didn't exist in the real world. They only existed in my mind but I didn't know that. I really thought they were all real and that I was undergoing a mysterious and unique psychic experience and calling from God through his holy spirit. Unfortunately, the truth was that I had mentally cracked up and needed psychiatric help immediately before my mental health deteriorated even further. Sadly, I had no idea that I was becoming mentally ill and that I was actually suffering from paranoid schizophrenia in reality. I needed to see a professional psychiatrist about the voices I was hearing in my head and the hallucinations that I was seeing, and to start taking anti-psychotic medication immediately to treat my mental illness. However, I didn't do that because I didn't know I was mentally ill. I needed urgent and immediate treatment for my mental illness. However, I thought the only explanation there was for what I was going through was that I must be possessed by the Devil and evil spirits or I was specially chosen by God to go on a holy, religious mission for him. Being haunted and tormented by the Devil and his evil spirits and not being able to see my daughter were the reasons why I had decided to leave London, and go and work for a language school in Istanbul, Turkey from the New Year, in January 1999. I believed that the house and rented room that I'd been living in must be haunted by the Devil and all the evil spirits and demons that I'd been seeing and hearing and that they might leave me alone, if I moved out and went somewhere else, for example to work in another country, like Turkey. I believed they would not be able to follow me.

I caught my flight to Istanbul on the 26th of December 1998 and arrived there on the same day. I was met at the airport by the brother of my new school's owner, and taken to my flat in the Fatih area of Istanbul, which was paid for by the school. The ghosts, demons and spirits weren't there and I started teaching in my new job, so all started off well. I was teaching again, which I was very happy about, and enjoying living in Istanbul. I decided that I would never smoke marijuana again. One of my very friendly Muslim students had given me a copy of the Koran in English in Istanbul, so I took it home and read it occasionally. However, a deep mental and emotional sadness and brokenness still persisted in my mind about my daughter and I burst into weeping and sobbing bouts for long periods of my spare time in my flat on a regular, daily basis.

Then one day in March 1999 when I'd been in Istanbul for a few months, Satan appeared to me in my living room, while I was reading the Bible. Then I heard and saw some angels talking about me above my head in the spiritual realm of heaven just below the ceiling of my living room. They opened the curtain of heaven to look down on Satan talking to me. He asked me: 'can I enter your circle', which I took to mean that he wanted to come into my life. Of course I said 'no'. He then disappeared through the front door to the flat. He looked so evil with eyes showing no emotion, and suddenly I became completely terrified and paranoid that he had found me and would now haunt my flat on a regular basis and try to persecute and possess me. Some days later, I saw a legion of evil spirits from the Bible jumping around in the living room of my flat and then I knew that my flat was becoming haunted by the Devil and his legions. They were coming out of a host evil spirit in the room and there were at least 6 of them jumping up and down, causing chaos and trying to scare and possess me. And scared I was, I was completely paranoid about being possessed by them and I was thoroughly convinced that the Bible was my only protection against all of these evil phenomena haunting me, so I retreated into my private bedroom to study it in all its entirety, in all my spare time. However, this was quickly turning me into a religious lunatic, but I still thought it could protect me against being possessed by Satan. The Devil and his evil legions from the Bible had followed me to Turkey. As time passed by I could still see and hear spirits haunting my main living room, so I tried to avoid going in there as much as possible.

Then one day while I was studying my Bible in my bedroom, I suddenly saw Moses come down from heaven through the walls of my room and he started talking to me. He told me that he had a message from God for me. He said my help was needed in heaven because Satan the Devil was trying to take over in heaven. I had to go around converting people on earth to be Catholics and baptizing them into the Catholic faith. This was my top secret mission from God. I quickly agreed that I would do this for God and thanked Moses for his message. Moses then disappeared back through the wall of my bedroom and went back up to heaven where I could see he was sitting next to God.

After Moses' visit to me in my bedroom, I became absolutely convinced that I had finally found out what I was supposed to be doing with my life that had been secretly revealed to me by Moses' message directly from God. I read the Bible some more and believed that I had to turn my whole life into a Catholic mission on earth for God. I would heal the sick, raise the dead, cast out demons and baptize people in the name of the father, the son and the holy ghost, as I had in my previous life on earth as Jesus, which I believed was who I really was. I then had flashes of religious inspiration and hope through the holy spirit. I was suddenly happy that I had been called on by God and that I finally had a reason for living on earth. I believed I had finally discovered the meaning of life and the meaning of everyone's lives. I knew now that God was real after all and that Catholicism was the one and only true religion. I was on the right path. I was in no doubt that the holy spirit was with me and protecting me on my holy mission for God. This was how convincing my schizophrenia was to me. It was deceiving me in my own mind. This is obviously why many sufferers of schizophrenia, myself included at the time, sometimes cannot fully acknowledge that they are suffering from mental illness.

I had started out in life as an atheist, coming from a family of atheists. Then I had travelled to Thailand where I was impressed by the peace and inner harmony message of Buddhism, so I converted to Buddhism while I was there. Then I moved onto Christianity in Thailand because I felt that the Bible filled what had been a huge gap in my intellectual and, if there is such a thing, a spiritual void in my life. In reality, the biggest gaps and voids were in my education and failing at my M.Ed dissertation had, arguably, hit my intellectual life and career hardest of all. When I was doing the dissertation, I had big plans for myself and my future career. I was going to be the best teacher at the schools I taught in, and in a few years I would progress into getting promoted to take on roles such as the head of a department or vice principal positions. After that, I could even someday have attained principal positions in schools I would work in, and settle down into a second marriage with a woman I really wanted to make a new life with. Now, all of my plans for career progression had simply gone out of the window.

The Revelation

Mostly, in between my occasional schizophrenic delusions, my life in 1999 in Istanbul passed peacefully. I still had long periods of sanity, which alternated with paranoid delusions. I had a very nice and comfortable rent free flat in a good area of the city. I took local buses to work each day to travel to the area of Besiktas, where my school was. My classes were going well and my students liked me. Then in June, I decided to look for a new job in Istanbul that paid more. I had my Dip.Ed certificate and an English teaching certificate from the University of London. I applied for the American school of Istanbul and got the job. The salary was better and I moved to a comfortable flat just outside of Uskudar, on the Asian side of the city. My life was improving. I went out to eat and drink at nice places and my classes were fine. My students all liked me and I was a very popular teacher at the school. I made friends with the school owner's son and he introduced me to his friends. I used to go out at night to play football with his friends every week and one of his friends took me to Galatasaray's home matches, so I became a Galatasaray fan. I started a British university teaching course in September and wrote a very good first assignment for the first module at the British Council library in Istanbul. The news came back that I had passed in December, so I felt happy at that time that I was getting my life back together and doing positive things.

In February 2000 in Istanbul, several months after seeing Moses come down from heaven into my bedroom to send me on a mission from God, I was walking home from school one day when I encountered a group of demons on a quiet street. Then the voice of an angel said to me, 'repeat after me': "I am the first and the last. I am he who liveth and was dead, and behold I am alive forever more, and hath the keys of hell and of death". I immediately recognized the verse from the book of Revelation and I repeated it to all the demons I was seeing. Then I saw huge balls of flame rise up in the street between me and the demons and separate the demons from myself. This holy verse and the balls of flame were sent for me by God to protect me from evil. The demons had all run away back down the street from which they came, because of the flames of fire from heaven. Then I saw angels in heaven flying across and above a nearby cemetery. As I looked into heaven, they were producing souls on the orders of God to be sent into all new babies who were being born on the earth. This was some more evidence that I had needed to carry on with my holy Catholic mission. After experiencing this event, I carried on walking home, deeply convinced about what I had witnessed.

On March the 10th 2000 as I was walking home for the night at about 9pm in Taksim Square in Istanbul, an angel descended from heaven and appeared to me to show me the full revelation of Saint John the Divine from the book of Revelation in the Bible. The angel hovered in front of me on a dark street corner and told me to look at a scene taking place in the street. As I looked at the street, I saw Satan flying around and calling to all his legions, demons and evil spirits to come out of all the bodies of the Turkish Muslim people they had possession of. Satan's legions obeyed him and I saw them all gather together to follow him flying around in the dark night sky just below heaven, from which bright lights were shining over the streets of Istanbul.

As I looked up at heaven, I saw the Catholic God and myself standing beside him surrounded by angels and light as the revelation unfolded. A trumpet was sounded by an angel in heaven and another angel read out judgment passages from the Bible about all the evil sinners in the world and how they were all condemned to eternal damnation in hell with Satan. This was listened to by all the angels and spirits around, including Satan and his legions. Satan flew over to stand in front of me and told me he was Allah. He then asked me who I chose to follow. When I pointed at the Catholic God I could see in heaven, he flew away back to his army of evil legions. The Catholic God gestured to Satan that Satan could have all the Muslim Turkish people as followers and the angel in front of me said: 'go home and read Mathew chapter 4'. Then I left and made my way home, convinced I was the second coming of Jesus Christ because I had seen myself in heaven and the Revelation was revealed only to me. I was also terribly paranoid that Satan might be following me everywhere and he could possess me at any time. I was living in constant fear and paranoia of possession by the Devil.

When I got home, I read Mathew chapter 4 in the Bible and it said: 'get thee hence Satan, for it is written: thou shalt worship the Lord thy God and him only shalt thou serve'. When I read this, I immediately became convinced and absolutely certain that I really was Jesus in the flesh, in the second coming, coming to judge the world, and fight the final conflict of good against evil with Satan, and defeat him. I studied the Koran at home too and compared it with the Bible. Whenever I found discrepancies between the two books, I blamed Satan's lies in the Koran for twisting the truth against the one true Catholic God. This was the conflict of good against evil, God against the Devil and Catholicism against Islam. I believed this was my top secret, spiritual mission, and spiritual awakening in life that had been revealed to me. This was definitely the final conflict as had been revealed to me in the revelation I had witnessed. The Catholic God and one and only true religion versus Satan and Islam: the false God Allah (the Devil) and false religion of Islam with all of its Devil possessed followers.

I became convinced then that Muhammad was the false prophet mentioned in the book of Revelation and Islam was the 666 beast. In a vision through the holy spirit, I had seen that the Devil's false religion of Islam was actually started by Satan with Muhammad in hell, in the year 666 (the mark of the beast) and that it was being used by Satan to brainwash his followers and take them down to hell, and to take the glory away from the Catholic God and religion. I realized I had a special mission in my life: Jesus' mission to heal the sick, raise the dead, judge people and to engage in a spiritual fight in the final conflict between God and Satan. I believed then that Satan had possessed all Muslims with his evil legions to take them all down to hell with, and through, the verses of the Koran. And that Catholicism was the one and only true religion in the world, as had been revealed to me by the angels of heaven in the revelation I saw through the holy spirit of God. Satan was being worshipped as Allah by Muslims everywhere and they really didn't know he was Satan and that Muhammad was the false prophet in the book of Revelation. I imagined that world war 3 between Catholics and Muslims was definitely going to happen and I was called by God on a top secret, religious mission to save the world from the destruction of Satan, the false God – Allah. Of course, in reality, these were all my paranoid, schizophrenic, persecutory delusions. Obviously, my mental illness was getting worse and worse.

I began to dress myself all in white – white Jacket, white shirt, white belt and white trousers, so that I would look like Jesus as described in the book of Revelation. I bought these items of clothing in Istiklal Caddessi, which was a high class shopping street in Istanbul. Then I felt I would be appropriately attired to do miracles and judge the world and all its sinners, sending them all down to eternal damnation in hell, which Jesus is supposed to do in the book of revelation, in which it is written that he has the keys of hell and of death. Therefore, I believed that I now also had this power. I had visions that it was time for me to reveal myself to the world as the 'Messiah', Jesus in the second coming as predicted in the book of Revelation and that this time, I had come not to be crucified but to judge all the world's sinners. This was what it was obviously all about! The evil spirits in the streets had also said to me several times: 'I know thee who thou art Jesus of Nazareth; thou art the Christ, the holy one of God'.

These were some of the imaginary, schizophrenic voices that I had heard in my mentally ill mind. To me, this was merely confirmation that I really was Jesus. I began to go to church regularly in Istanbul, which I believed would protect me from being possessed by Satan. And to protect myself in my flat, I bought about 50 crosses at the church, which I hung around my flat in every available space, so that Satan and his legions couldn't attack me or possess me at home. I started to go out around Istanbul regularly at night to drive out demons and evil spirits from the streets, which I could clearly see through God's holy spirit. I visited churches to pray deeply, when I had been an atheist for most of my life, until I had gone to Thailand and converted to Buddhism there. Finally, I left my teaching job in Istanbul and traveled to Rome, Italy where I hoped to live in the Vatican as the new Pope, and be recognized as Jesus. My schizophrenic delusions were going from bad to worse. Imagining that I was Jesus and that I was going to be the next Pope were just two of the grandiose delusions that I was suffering from with my schizophrenia.

However, when I arrived at the airport in Rome, there was no meeting party to greet me and recognize me from the Vatican, so I shouted 'I'm God' in the middle of the airport in Rome and I was escorted out of the airport by the Italian airport police. I then decided to travel to the Philippines and live there because it was a Catholic country, where I believed I would be protected from Satan and his legions. I determined that I would fly to Bangkok first, and fly to the Philippines from there, so I bought a ticket to Bangkok in Rome in May 2000. When I landed in Bangkok, I found that I was ignored there at the airport too, so people obviously didn't recognize me as the second coming of Jesus, which I became very angry about. However, I booked myself into a hotel on Khao San Road in Bangkok, where I could see and hear all manner of spirits and aliens, who were in continuous verbal and psychic, spiritual communication with me. One of the spirits told me that I would receive a $100 million contract to make a film about my life, when I landed in the Philippines. Another spirit told me that the Philippine government would meet me at the airport, and take me to a palace, which they would give me, where I could live comfortably and safely in peace for the rest of my life.

Then when I went out onto the street, I could see aliens flying around in flying saucers up and down the street on orders from the Devil. They were invading the world from outer space to help the Devil. So I bought my flight ticket to the Philippines and when I arrived at the airport expecting my $100 million for a film about my life, a grand public reception and a palace from the government, I found that I was completely ignored again and that nobody even noticed me. Finally, after sleeping at the airport for 2 nights I reluctantly bought a flight ticket back to London. It was lucky that I did because I could get the mental health treatment that I really desperately needed in London, which I didn't know that I needed.

I believed that the CIA, FBI, KGB and British MI5 were following me around, and trying to capture me because I had the power of God to heal the sick, cleanse lepers, tread on serpents and raise the dead. I could also part the sea and turn water into wine, as well as do other miracles, such as communicate with the dead and the spirit world, which I believed I was doing all the time. I believed I had parted the Bosphorus Sea in Istanbul to prove my faith in God. As the secret service agencies were desperate to abuse the power of God, which I obviously had, for their own selfish national interests, I was continually having to keep a low profile in public, so that they couldn't capture me and take me prisoner. The CIA, FBI, MI5 and KGB wanted to use the power of God to control the world. These were all part of the paranoid, persecutory delusions that I was suffering from. The secret services wanted to acquire the power of God from me, in order to be able to manufacture more nuclear weapons to blow the world up with. That was Satan's evil plan: to destroy the world and it was part of my holy mission to stop him.

This, then, was the situation when I arrived at Heathrow airport in London in June 2000. I didn't want to return to my mother's because I thought she would be in cahoots with MI5, so I slept on sofas at Heathrow airport for 3 days. On the fourth day, 2 police officers came up to me, interviewed me and took me away from Heathrow in the back of a police van. I had told them that I was Jesus Christ and the holy ghost, all in one. I was terribly paranoid that they were taking me to a secret MI5 interrogation centre to be interrogated about the power of God, which, obviously, I alone on earth knew how to command. The police drove the van through the streets for about 15 minutes, until we arrived at Hillingdon hospital, where they stopped the van outside the psychiatric unit. When they took me out of the van and into the psychiatric unit, I knew that MI5 were planning to brainwash me on the 'psychiatric' ward. The KGB were waiting to talk to me outside the hospital, to get me on their side.

Real Life and Recovery

I was interviewed by 'doctors' on the ward, whom I told that MI5, the CIA, the KGB and the FBI were after me for my power of God. I also told one doctor who interviewed me that my name was Jesus and that I was the holy ghost, who walks in the midst of the 7 golden candlesticks from the book of revelation. The doctor told me that he was detaining me under section 1 of the mental health act for 1 month. I said I had to leave the 'hospital' immediately because the KGB were following me and I refused to stay there. The staff then forcefully injected me with drugs, which made me fall unconscious and I woke up hours later on a hospital bed. When I got up and tried to leave the psychiatric ward, I was told that I wasn't allowed to leave and I found that all the doors and windows to the outside were locked. On my second day, the staff took me downstairs to the more open ward, where most patients weren't troublesome at all and I was glad I was considered one of them.

Life on the psychiatric ward seemed to be quite good for people who were mentally ill, apart from the fact that I was incarcerated 24 hours a day, 7 days a week. There were three very good meals a day from a canteen near another ward in the hospital, which one could walk to in about 2 minutes. Patients each had separate beds, of course, in different dormitory rooms. There was a living room with a television in it. There was also a telephone on the ward for patients who wanted to talk to friends and family outside the hospital. The doctors got in touch with my family and they brought me some food and cigarettes, so at least I could pass the time smoking in the smoking room on the ward. Every evening there were nurses giving out medication, which one had to take. The first time they called out 'medication' to me and I told them I didn't need it, I was then quickly surrounded by 6 staff who all held me down on my bed and forcefully injected me with depixol - an anti-psychotic drug. They also gave me other drugs to take - 2 pills a day, which were also anti-psychotic. I found out that the doctors were forcefully, legally, detaining me on the psychiatric ward for my own good and safety. And, in my sane mind, I now agree with their decision and I'm glad they did it. One of the doctors told me that I had a chemical imbalance in my brain and that they were giving me anti – psychotic medication to balance my brain chemicals out into the right places again.

Daily life on the ward usually started at about 7 am, when patients were woken up for breakfast. We then walked to the canteen where we could have cereal and milk with toast and jam. It was all provided buffet style. Patients usually talked together as they ate breakfast but one could tell that some patients, me included, were very ill. Breakfast usually went on until about 9 am and it was good to go to the canteen for all meals, even if one wasn't that hungry. It gave patients a break from sitting on the ward all day with nothing to do. Patients were also allowed to smoke in a sitting room adjacent to the canteen, after breakfast, so many patients did this while they sat down and chatted. After breakfast, everyone had to go back to the ward, where they could sit in the living room and watch television, sit in the smoking room and smoke or go to their bedrooms. The routines for lunch and dinner were the same. It was all very monotonous but one looked forward to all the meal times because they broke up the day and added some routine to it. It was all dreadfully boring and dull, and time passed very, very slowly with virtually nothing to do but sit and wait to get out of the hospital – to be discharged. I mostly sat in the smoking room and smoked through the day with the other patients there. A patient told me that several people wanted to commit suicide and that others had schizophrenia, which made me terrified. A patient strolled around on the ward saying, 'forgive me Lord' continually and other patients smoked cannabis in their bedrooms, which they had obviously smuggled onto the ward.

I had some money saved up from my teaching job, so I was able to send one of the staff out of the hospital to a shop, to buy some rolling tobacco for myself, which helped to get me through my time in hospital. Occasionally, I would sit in the living room to watch television, read newspapers or magazines or talk to other patients. Nobody wanted to be there and most patients were just looking forward to being discharged. I attended a computer class in hospital, in which I typed up a C.V, in order to get myself a job when I was finally able to leave the hospital. As the weeks passed, I was allowed out to visit my family at home in the Holland Park area of London, which was at least an hour's journey from Hillingdon hospital, where I was being detained. I used to travel there on the London underground. I got a lot out of these visits and the medication I was on, and the hearing of voices and having hallucinations stopped completely, in time.

When my full month was up on the ward, I was fortunately discharged to my family and to my local doctor in Holland Park, so that I could continue getting my regular anti-psychotic medication from him and continue to recover. These injections of Depixol had worked, as my symptoms of schizophrenia, hearing voices, having hallucinations and paranoid, persecutory delusions, had stopped. I then became extremely depressed because I realized I wasn't Jesus after all, I didn't have a job, and didn't have any money. These realities about my life were very depressing. I also wasn't sure that I had become mentally ill – I thought perhaps I had just had a major nervous and mental breakdown because of all my stresses from not seeing my daughter and missing her. It was depressing too to realize that I wasn't going to live in a palace, nobody was going to make a film about my life and I wouldn't live a life of luxury at the Vatican as the Pope. The doctors weren't yet calling my illness schizophrenia – it was psychosis and I had just had my first psychotic episode.

While I was in Istanbul, Turkey in 1999, I was accepted onto a British university's M.A course in teaching English, so I now resumed my studies on module 2 of the programme, in my spare time in London, in September 2000. I had completed module 1 in Istanbul. I knew I had to get back to work to have any chance of a normal life again after my mental breakdown, which was what I called it, so I set about updating my C.V and I went around London to visit several language schools to look for English teaching work. With my diploma in Education and my certificate in teaching English, I was offered a teaching position at a school in Finsbury Park on Seven Sisters Road, to start in January 2001, for 7 pounds an hour. Of course, I immediately took the job and started teaching there in January 2001. I had also applied to my local council to be put on their housing waiting list with all of the housing points I had accrued by being struck down with my mental illness. While I was waiting for permanent housing, I was staying at a hostel run by a charity for sufferers with mental health problems on St. Mark's Road just off Ladbroke Grove.

So in 2001, after my first breakdown, I had a regular, positive and constructive purpose and routine for my life and recovery in London. I was working full time at my school in Finsbury Park from 9am to 4pm, I was then traveling to the university of London institute of Education library, near Russell Square and studying there from 4.30 pm to 9 pm every evening and I was going to the doctor's once a month to pick up my prescriptions for my Olanzapine anti-psychotic medication to keep myself mentally healthy. My studies had been going well and they helped to mentally bring me back to the reality of the real world and focus on my real life in the here and now. I completed module 2 of my course and I was progressing to module 3. After finishing module 3, I would be half way through my Master's degree. That was real progress. My students at school were mostly Turkish and as I had been teaching in Turkey, we had a lot to talk about, and got on very well together. We used to go out to a local café in Finsbury Park together at break times, and have breakfast together. Mostly, we just chatted as friends and their English improved consistently.

My routine at the university of London library was to arrive there at about 4.30 pm every week day and then to pile the teaching books onto my desk that I needed to read and make reference to, for my latest assignments. I was reading approximately 3 teaching books a week and attending lectures part time on week nights. At weekends, I was usually studying hard at the library, reading and writing essays from 10.30 am until 5 pm. I took my daughter there occasionally, so that she could read the vast collection of children's books that they had there. My daughter was having a good time with me again and I was regularly taking her to the cinema to see children's films, whenever I had odd weekends off studying. Module 3 went well and I handed in all my completed assignments to the university, on time as usual. I felt I was growing in confidence and I was happy that my life seemed to be going smoothly again. My relationship at school with my boss was good and she liked me, and was pleased with my teaching work and the positive feedback that I got from my students.
In about August of 2001, when I was waiting to start my 4th module of my M.A, I received a new class of Brazilian students at my school. They were all trainee Brazilian pastors, who had come to London on a

religious mission for their church - the universal church of the kingdom of God, which was established in the old Apollo theatre in Finsbury Park on Seven Sister's Road. I taught the pastors English as usual, and made friends with them. They told me that their mission was to help people, and do miracles for people in the church and they asked me if I was interested in being converted by them and attending their church. I told them that I didn't believe in it and so they dropped their suggestions for me.

Relapse 1

In spite of having been obviously mentally ill during my first psychotic episode, I still didn't deeply believe that I might have a mental illness. What would anyone's reaction be, if they were told they were mentally ill? Deep inside myself, I still thought that I had had a psychic, spiritual and profoundly religious awakening and experience. This opinion of mine led me to stop taking my medication after about a year of having done so, since my discharge from hospital in July 2000. I had asked the doctor and my social worker how long I would have to take it for and they both said 'a year', so after a year I stopped taking it in September 2001. After all, I was normal again, wasn't I? I was living a normal life and no longer had any psychotic symptoms. The voices, hallucinations and delusions had stopped, so I thought, 'why not stop taking the pills'? I told myself, 'I'm better, I'm cured, I'm not mentally ill anymore'. Why should I continue taking the pills, when I thought I didn't need to? I felt better, believed I was well and stopped taking the pills. I convinced myself that I had only had a nervous breakdown and it wasn't actually a mental illness after all. I was still working full time, teaching the Brazilian pastors every day and travelling to university to study in the evenings as usual. My life was going well and I had completely recovered from whatever it was that I had gone through the last year.

I was studying at university one night, after I had stopped taking the pills for about 2 weeks, when angels began to appear to me again from heaven above my head and told me I had to go on a Catholic pilgrimage to France, Spain and Portugal because these were the nearest Catholic countries in Europe. They said I had to go to spread the word of God and use the power of God to perform the miracles of casting out evil spirits, casting out demons and raising the dead, which convinced me again that I really could do all of those things. They said the Vatican would then recognize me as Jesus of Nazareth in the second coming to judge the world. They also told me that Allah really was Satan and that he was gathering troops together to fight the final conflict for power in the world with the Catholic God and his believers. They also told me that the Vatican had been infiltrated by Satan, so Catholics now also believed that Satan was really God and I was the chosen one to rescue the world from Satan's lies against the one true God. As a result of this holy message from heaven, I resigned from my English teaching job in Finsbury Park, and went to Victoria bus station to buy bus tickets to Paris and Lisbon, with the intention of performing miracles everywhere along the way with my power of God. My schizophrenia had returned.

Before I went to France, the angels' voices told me to go to the universal church of the kingdom of God in Finsbury Park, where the Brazilian pastors were, and to put new crosses of Jesus, which I had recently bought, all around the inside of the building. So I set off for the church, the day before I had decided to travel to Paris. When I got to the church, I went inside and left many crucifixes there as a secret message from the angels to my Brazilian pastor students. I saw one of my students inside the church and I waved to him. He acknowledged me but didn't say anything. Then, I went back to my room in west London and prepared myself to go to France.

The next day, I packed a rucksack with my Bible and some crucifixes, and went to Victoria bus station in London, to get the first bus I could to Paris. On the bus I prayed continually for God to use me to heal the sick, raise the dead and to drive out spirits everywhere along the route of the bus. Once we arrived in Paris, I left the bus station to walk around Paris and perform miracles.

Everywhere I went in Paris, I believed I was driving out spirits and demons that had possessed people and that I was raising the dead from all the church cemeteries I visited. Finally, exhausted, I found a park and I slept rough in the freezing cold of the night in Paris. When I finally found a taxi driver who could take me back to the bus station in Paris, my bus to Lisbon had already gone and I had to buy another ticket. So I bought a ticket for another bus, which would leave that evening. This time I boarded the bus to Lisbon, as I had already done my holy work for God of performing countless miracles around the streets of Paris. When I arrived in Lisbon, the angels told me to get another bus to a holiday resort in the south of Portugal. I did what God had commanded me to do through the angels and I waited patiently at the bus station in Lisbon for the next bus to Faro, which is in the south of Portugal. The bus journey was uneventful except for the angels telling me continually to heal the sick, raise the dead and to drive out demons everywhere I went. The voices of the angels were now in almost complete control of my whole life.

When I arrived in Faro, the angels told me which hotel to stay in, where to eat, what to eat and what to do. Once I had checked into my hotel I was ordered to walk continuously around the town performing miracles and proving my faith in God. The angels told me one night to lie down next to some railway tracks with a train coming along, and stay there until it had passed. I did exactly as they asked and the train went harmlessly by. I now believed that I had proved myself to the angels and that I had passed their and God's test of my religious, Catholic faith. I now believed that God was guiding me and protecting me in everything I did. Finally, after a week of performing miracles in Faro, or so I believed, the angels told me to go back to Lisbon and from there to take a train to Madrid. I was listening and talking to the angels continually on the bus back to Lisbon and on the train to Madrid. The schizophrenic voices, hallucinations and delusions were as bad as ever.

When I arrived in Madrid, the angels told me to go out walking around and perform miracles there, which I did. Then they told me to get a train to Barcelona and from there another train to Lloret De Mar on the coast. The angels were now sending me messages all the time and I continually had to look up above my own head into heaven, to make sure I was receiving their messages loud and clear. When I got to Lloret, I checked into the hotel that the angels told me to, and had a swim at the beach. Then I spent my days casting out demons and legions, which had possessed people, and which habitually attached themselves to places of sin such as pubs, bars, discos and nightclubs. So I would frequent these places, just as Jesus did, to drive out Satan's evil forces and influences. In the evenings, I would visit these places for a beer and a meal and then command all evil spirits to leave and not return. When I had cleansed a place, I didn't need to go back to it but I would visit other different places, which were also possessed and haunted, the next night and so forth. Sometimes the angels told me to leave my hotel room in the middle of the night, and walk through the countryside to deserted forests, and to cast out demons there in those dark, evil places, which I did. I didn't see or hear from the Devil anymore, just angels and spirits. The angels were sending me messages from God all day and all night.

Finally, I had run out of money to pay for my hotel and for food, so I became a homeless, roaming tramp, and walked through quiet countryside to look for a main road, from which I could hitch a lift to Barcelona. And I got lucky when I was picked up by a kindly Spaniard, who was traveling to Barcelona, who dropped me off at the British embassy there. From the British embassy, I called my mother and persuaded her to send me enough money for a flight ticket back to Britain, which she fortunately did. My flight was from Barcelona to Luton airport and I hitched another lift from someone to get back into London from the airport. He dropped me at an underground station in north London. I walked through north and central London casting out spirits and demons all the way, until I made it back through west London to my hostel off Ladbroke Grove. After a day back in my hostel room, the police, social services and some doctors came round and sectioned me under section 3 of the mental health act. This meant they could forcefully detain me in hospital for my own good for 6 months. They asked me what my name was and I told them, 'Jesus'. Then they asked me who my mother was and I answered, 'Mary'. They asked me what I could tell them about the struggle between good and evil and I told them that Satan was Allah and that Islam was his false religion. So they took me away to hospital in an ambulance, and checked me into a psychiatric ward at St. Charles' hospital near Ladbroke Grove.

Treatment

Once I was back on the psychiatric ward, the doctors told me I needed to go back to taking my anti-psychotic medication of olanzapine immediately again, regularly every day for at least the next 5 years. They made it clear that if I didn't comply with this order, I wouldn't be allowed out of the ward or out of hospital again, until I did. So every day at medication time I would comply with their order of taking 10 milligrams of olanzapine, and the voices of angels and spirits and the hallucinations of God, angels, demons and evil spirits slowly began to disappear. I went to the weekly ward rounds to talk to the doctors about my psychiatric experiences, where I admitted that I had stopped taking my medication and, as a result of this, I had become unwell again. I admitted that I had had hallucinations and heard voices, which had deluded me and that I had had paranoid persecutory delusions that I was Jesus in the second coming and that the FBI, CIA, KGB and MI5 were after me to steal the power of God from me. I also told the doctors that I thought I had been on a holy mission to spread the word of God and to defeat the Devil.

The doctors and social workers were pleased that I had faced up to, and told, the truth about my psychotic illness because having insights into one's mental illness is the first step to recovery. Obviously, if one knows one is mentally ill, one is likely to take the medication, and not to become ill again. However, if the person is in denial, he is less likely to take the medication and, therefore, fall ill again. I had been admitted to the ward in November 2001 and I was discharged 6 weeks later in December 2001, just before Christmas, because I had insight into my illness and because I was taking my medication regularly again, which had made me well again. At that stage, the doctors still weren't saying that

I had schizophrenia, although they did convey to me that they thought it could be. Instead, they were still saying that it was psychosis, which was a symptom of schizophrenia.

Life on the psychiatric ward had been good. One slept in a dormitory with one's own individual bed and cupboard. There were regular, weekly meetings with the doctors in a private room, where patients could discuss their problems and the doctors could assess the patients and their individual situations. There were weekly classes for patients to pass the time with, such as cookery, drawing, and painting and there were also quizzes for patients' rest and recreation. For the rest of the time, patients could watch television in a lounge, listen to music, chat, and use the gym, read books or newspapers or sit and smoke, while drinking tea or coffee on comfortable sofas in a lounge. I had made several friends on the ward who also had schizophrenia, so I often sat and talked to them. There were 3 meals a day on the ward and each patient generally had to use their time on the ward to take their medication and develop insight into their illness, in order to make a full recovery. Everything on the ward was in place to provide patients with all the rest and recreation they needed to recover. While I was in hospital I was informed that I had been awarded a studio flat on a local estate with all the housing points I had accrued by becoming mentally ill for a second time, so when I was discharged from hospital in December 2001, I was able to move straight into my new flat.

I decided to renew my M.A studies with my university, and to re-apply for my teaching job in Finsbury Park. I got lucky. My school took me back to teach full time again and I was now past the halfway mark on my M.A course. So, now living in my own flat, I was able to resume my daily routine of teaching at school from 9am to 4pm and then studying at the University of London every weekday evening from 5pm to 9pm and from 10am to 5pm every Saturday and Sunday. I got myself well quickly by continuing with my medication, and tried to sort myself and my life out mentally and emotionally.

My routine went well again in 2002 and definitely helped me to get back into real, normal life, and to recover from my second bout of mental illness. I would wake up every day at 7am, take a quick bath and catch the underground from Ladbroke Grove to Finsbury Park at around 8am. Most of my students were friendly, Brazilian, Turkish and eastern European people, who had come to London with the sole intention of improving their English to get better paying jobs back in their own countries. As I had been teaching for many years by that time, I was at an advantage over other teachers teaching them, because I understood their culture, motivations and could relate to them well from my experiences teaching abroad. We would often take cigarette and coffee breaks together and my friendly relations with them certainly made my job of teaching them easier and more enjoyable. In time, my students and I became good friends, which made me happy because it meant my job was more secure. Once my afternoon classes finished at 4pm every day, I would rush off again to the underground and take the train to the University of London's institute of Education library, where I would study every evening and night from about 4.30pm until 9pm when the Education library closed. The Education library was the best place in London for me to go to, to complete my M.A studies, because it had more than one thousand professional and academic books and journals on teaching English.

I was acutely aware that my M.A studies and paying the rent for my flat all hinged on my job at the school, so I crawled, begged and groveled to keep my job with my bosses there, whenever I saw them. Fortunately for me, I made it through to finishing my dissertation for my M.A degree, and submitted it to the university in January 2003, after working on it for 1 whole year. It was 20,000 words long and I'd read over 100 books and journals to complete it. While I was working on finishing my M.A degree throughout 2002, I'd had no other life apart from my teaching at the school in Finsbury Park. I had no friends, girlfriends or any social life throughout the year. That was the sacrifice I'd had to make for my M.A. However, I used to see my daughter at least once a month to take her out to the cinema.

A New Life?

Now, in January 2003 with my M.A completed, I started to look for jobs abroad again in Asia. I applied for, and got, a management job with my M.A as a director of studies with a language school in Jakarta, Indonesia. I was to move to Jakarta in February 2003 to take up my post. I was really thrilled that the M.A had earned me a well-paid management job with a reputable school. However, I knew I still needed to take my daily, anti-psychotic olanzapine medication, so I persuaded my doctor to prescribe me with a year's supply before I left. Finally, it was time to leave in February 2003. My daughter was very upset about it but I had made up my mind that the job opportunities were better for me overseas, so that was where I had to be to have a successful career and a better life. In addition, my ex-wife and my mother had always been bitter and spiteful to me over my daughter, so I decided that it was better to be far away from them and to live a new, happy life away from all of those problems. I had decided that I definitely needed to start a new life for myself abroad.

My new life in Jakarta started well as soon as I got there. I was taken to my new, 3 bedroom, 3 storey house in a peaceful and quiet central Jakarta neighborhood and I was shown my new office at the school, which I'd be working from. I decided then that because I was now such a successful person, I obviously hadn't been mentally ill after all and that, therefore, I no longer needed to take my medication any more. My new found success at finishing my M.A degree and becoming the new manager of a school convinced me that I didn't need to take any more medication. My life was going well again. I had finally got myself an excellent university education and a successful management position. There was no need for me to take medication after all and my previous life had just been one big mistake. Perhaps that was why I had needed medication in the past – because of my mistakes in my old life. No such worries now as I was such a resounding success in, and at, life. My M.A had suddenly sky rocketed me to success in one giant leap.

My new job started off very well. I wrote curricula, observed teachers, ran teacher training workshops and also had a teaching timetable. I was friendly and got on well with all the teachers, school staff and students. Many of the students invited me out to have dinner with them and to join them for other social occasions. Rini, one of my several Indonesian girlfriends, found me a new house to share with her, near the teaching centre in central Jakarta and she also took care of all the furniture shopping and neighborhood hassles for me. It was wonderful to have girlfriends – I was sleeping with different women every week, enjoying alcohol, bars, restaurants and nightclubs every night. My social life was fantastic and it really helped me to unwind, relax and recover my mind after I'd been slogging away at university for years on my M.A. I met so many really beautiful, Indonesian women, and slept with as many as I could, to forget about my failed marriage, and to make up for the fact that I wasn't seeing my daughter. All the beautiful women became therapy for me. I believed that all of the women I was sleeping with were helping me to recover from the broken marriage I'd had with my Thai ex-wife, and from the mental and emotional trauma I'd had from not having equal access to my daughter.

My teaching was going really well too. I usually taught between 18 and 25 hours a week to private groups of individuals or to private company classes. My students and I got on very well together and they would often invite me out to restaurants with them or to their private homes for meals. I had virtually the best routine I had ever had. I would normally start teaching at around 8am, and stay at the office until 5pm. After that I would go home, change into casual clothes and then go out for the night to meet any of my current girlfriends. I would usually go eating and drinking first, at a bar or restaurant in the block M area of Jakarta, and then go to a nightclub afterwards to meet women. My life continued happily like this for all of 2003 and I also visited Bali for my holidays. This was definitely the happiest time of my life so far, and I could forget about my bitterness with my ex-wife, and being unable to see my daughter any more. Instead of traumatizing about those things, I now had total happiness in my life again for the first time since I had got divorced 5 years ago. There were several Indonesian girlfriends that I had that I was madly in love with but the problem was that I didn't want to get married again, after my own first failed marriage in the past. This was definitely a factor which made me think that I couldn't spend my life with any of the women I met, who were much better for me than my ex-wife. I thought I was too scared of going through any more mental and emotional trauma to get married for a second time.

Then, in January 2004, I took a job to teach in west Papua province, in the farthest eastern part of Indonesia. The job was to teach English to a high ranking official and a group of his colleagues and staff. I really wanted to travel in Indonesia, so I accepted the teaching post there. It meant living there, away from Jakarta and the modern world for about 6 months. Someone once said of Papua that, 'it is the last wilderness on earth', and this was why I really wanted to see it. There were still tribes there, whose culture was unchanged from stone age times and I thought that was fascinating. The flights over eastern Indonesia revealed the most stunning geographical beauty to me. There were beautiful, sparsely inhabited and uninhabited islands glistening in the sun, in the midst of   vast swathes of empty ocean with the most beautiful natural scenery I had ever seen. They had fantastic beaches, mountains and volcanoes on them with no people living there. And I felt very excited and privileged to be one of the few people to see eastern Indonesia and to visit west Papua.

When I arrived in west Papua, I was given special and very privileged treatment. I was met at the airport in Sorong and moved immediately into a 5 star hotel with all expenses paid for. The classroom was a luxurious room on the roof of the hotel and I taught there every afternoon from 1pm to 5pm. And that was how great my life was in west Papua. I lived in the lap of luxury with all expenses paid for by my VIP students. In my time off, I would visit a remote sandy beach where I would go swimming in the sea every day and at weekends, and meet the local, indigenous Papuan people. Then one day in my 5 star hotel, while I was having breakfast, I met a beautiful Indonesian woman called Shanti. She was from Sulawesi and she told me that her mother had been a beauty queen. I fell in love with her and invited her to go out with me immediately. We quickly took to each other and became boyfriend and girlfriend, going out on dates regularly at night. Shanti then started visiting me in my room every night, and staying with me all of the nights of her remaining stay in west Papua. Obviously, she wanted to get married and I decided that I did too. Then at the end of my first month's teaching, I had a contract break to have a week's holiday in Bali. While I was staying in my hotel in Bali in February 2004 away from Shanti, I started to have paranoid delusions and hallucinations again. By this time, it had been more than a year since I had last taken my anti-psychotic medication.

Relapse 2

I had taken plenty of pills to west Papua, just in case I fell ill again out there, but I hadn't been taking any regularly. I had kept them in a drawer in my hotel room. However, now that I was becoming ill again, I didn't recognize it, and so still didn't take any of them to keep myself well. Then I got a phone call from my manager at the school in Jakarta, saying that I was not to go back to west Papua, but was to return to Jakarta instead because there had been an earthquake in west Papua and so it was no longer safe for me to be there. I reluctantly agreed to return to Jakarta the next week because of the earthquake. Meanwhile, in Bali, I was becoming more and more paranoid and delusional. I was having a massive mood swing of paranoia in my mind. My paranoia was that the Indonesian government in Jakarta were practicing political, policies of genocide on the native west Papuans. They had a transmigration policy in place where native Indonesians were migrating to west Papua to live and work, therefore excluding west Papuans from adequate housing and employment with which to live in their own, native province. I believed that the Indonesian military were colonizing the west Papuans and imprisoning them for trying to organize a free west Papua political, independence movement. This movement wanted to free west Papua from Indonesian rule and control.

Everywhere I had been in west Papua, I had seen displaced native west Papuans and their children who did not have equal opportunities with the native Indonesians to housing and employment. It was a racist policy of excluding west Papuans from equality with native Indonesians in their own province. Then I believed that MI5 were using me and my school to persecute the west Papuans too, by supporting the Indonesian colonists in west Papua by teaching English to them, while the average west Papuan was starving. This was how my third psychotic episode started out and these were the paranoid, persecutory delusions I was having. Of course, I was a mess with all of this on my holiday in Bali. I sat in my hotel room for hours sobbing about the Indonesian genocide of the west Papuans, which I imagined I was involved in by teaching English to the Indonesians there. My paranoid delusions had started up again.

When I got back to Jakarta, the angels of heaven were waiting for me to talk to me in my house. I believed that my delusions were the truth because I had read west Papuan reports of their Independence movement and the Indonesian military's persecution of them on their website of koteka.net. Consequently, I decided to leave my school because I believed I was being used by MI5. The angels told me to check into a 5 star hotel and to get a flight out of Jakarta to Bangkok, which I did. Then from Bangkok they told me to fly to Athens in Greece, which I also did. I arrived in Greece in April 2004, and checked into a budget hotel for 20 Euros a night in downtown Athens. In my hotel room, the angels told me that I was to visit every religious place in Greece and that I would soon be paid 100 million euros by someone coming to visit me. They told me that mother Mary was my real mother and that I was on a holy, religious, pilgrimage mission in Greece. I also made commands to all the angels for new biblical laws and rules throughout the world, as the new King of the world.

However, I soon ran out of money to pay for my hotel room, so I told the owner that my holy mother Mary would come to pay for me and he consequently took me down to the local police station and demanded money in front of the police. When I paid him all the money that I had and walked out onto the street, I was both penniless and homeless from that point onwards. This was in May

2004. The angels told me to walk out of Athens through forests and over hills into a small countryside town 20 - 30 kilometers away, which I did. When I got to the town, I found an empty, abandoned shop to live in. I slept there for a month, while I lived on food, drink and cigarettes from rubbish bins I would search, to stay alive.

Now I was a homeless tramp. In the space of 2 months with paranoid schizophrenia, I had resigned from my 5 star, all expenses paid, teaching life with a beautiful woman I wanted to marry in Indonesia, to become a homeless, starving, penniless, suffering, freezing cold tramp in the Greek countryside. Paranoid schizophrenia was destroying everything in my whole life. After staying in the abandoned shop in the small Greek town for a month, I found a mountain bike, which I rode back to Athens on. I rode around Athens for a few days living on waste food from restaurant tables, and picking up long cigarettes butts from the streets. Finally, the angels told me to ride into the countryside, and go up north to carry out a religious pilgrimage throughout all the holy sites in Greece.

I agreed with the angels, and rode out of Athens on my mountain bike. I found that I could cover about 50 kilometers per day, and whenever I came to fruit trees growing by the sides of the roads, I would eat as much fruit as I could. Whenever I passed through towns or cities, I would check all the rubbish bins for thrown away food. Sometimes I was lucky. Some bins had half eaten kebabs, pastries, chips, sandwiches and pizzas in them, so that was how I survived my holy pilgrimage through the whole of Greece to the northern city of Thessalonika. I arrived in Thessalonika in June 2004, after approximately 6 weeks of riding through Greece with the angels telling me where to go and what to do throughout my journey. The nights were freezing cold though, and I was starving along the way for much of the time, when I couldn't find any rubbish bins with food in them. I wouldn't have survived some of the nights in the cold, if I hadn't sometimes kept cycling all night, because that was what kept my body temperature warm on the freezing nights.

Rubbish bins, and begging at churches and farms along the way was how I had managed to survive for food. But I believed that, because I was Jesus on a holy pilgrimage, I had to endure some holy suffering. And this belief was really what kept me going throughout my pilgrimage. I believed the voices of the angels who told me that I was on a holy mission. Along the way throughout my ride to Thessalonika in the north, there were many churches and religious shrines and the angels told me to always stop at these to pray, light incense and meditate, which I always did. As I believed this would keep God with me. I thought that was the purpose of my journey and that God really had a plan for me. The angels told me that I had had to leave south-east Asia because the Muslims in Pakistan were going to nuclear bomb it all to start world war 3 for Allah, who was really Satan, against all other religions. I was absolutely convinced that this was the truth because I knew Satan wanted to start world war 3 between Muslims and Christians. Another thing that convinced me of my delusions was that I knew God and his angels wouldn't lie to me, so I did, and followed, everything they said.

Once I had arrived in Thessalonika, the angels told me to sleep on a park bench in the freezing cold, which I did for 2 nights. However, that didn't feel safe, so I decided to walk around the city, and try to find an abandoned building to live in. I got lucky. On a main street, I found an abandoned shop with a broken window. I climbed through the hole in the window, and had a look around. I went up the stairs inside, and found a room with a door, which I could close to sleep in, and in which I would be safe and warm. So I lived in the abandoned shop for a while. I felt warm and safe in there, protected from the dangers of the street. Once I had slept in there solidly for 2 days and 2 nights out of exhaustion from my journey, I ventured out onto the streets of Thessalonika to rummage in all the dustbins around the city, for food, drinks and cigarettes.

I established a routine of sleeping in the room of the abandoned shop all day and then walking through the streets to rummage in dustbins at night. And I must say I got very lucky. The abandoned shop was very clean and safe and I recovered from my 6 week mountain biking journey to Thessalonika with lots of sleep, because I hadn't been able to sleep well at nights on the journey. Sleeping rough in the freezing cold at night had left me with a number of long term aches and pains and cuts and bruises. The dustbins in Thessalonika are what kept me alive there for 7 months living as a filthy, freezing, starving, homeless tramp. I hadn't had a proper wash, bath or shower since I'd been on the road, when I'd washed in the streams, rivers and lakes that I had passed by. I had a route in Thessalonika of walking by all the restaurants, cafes and bars to pick up all the discarded food, drinks and cigarettes. Sometimes there would be portions of chips in containers, pizzas in boxes or sandwiches in wrappers, which all kept me alive. There were also lots of cups and bottles, half full of discarded soft drinks, including coffee and tea. Then there were the bags of popcorn along the promenade route and the sweet pancakes outside some late night cafes.

A good night was one in which I would find an assortment of food to take back to my room and discarded packets of cigarettes, so I would sit down on public benches around the city eating, drinking coffee and smoking cigarettes all night. Ironically, following the voices from heaven was part of what seemed to be keeping me alive. This is because I still believed that I was on a top secret, holy, pilgrimage of a mission to defeat Satan. And I believed this was why I had to suffer like Jesus as a homeless tramp. I also picked up some warm clothes to wear at a nearby church, which was not far from my abandoned shop home. I picked up some jeans, sweaters, shoes and a warm winter jacket from the church. Soon it was winter and the temperature dropped to below freezing in Thessalonika. One day in January 2005, the angels' voices told me to walk out of Thessalonika, along the coast to try to find an abandoned summer house to live in, which may have been abandoned for the winter.

I walked about 10 kilometers along the coast, to a small town called Nea Epivates, and got into an abandoned house, which had clearly been abandoned for the winter, as I had thought. It was facing the beach and all the shutters were down and locked. I went round to the back of the house, where there was a glass door with a key still in it. So I was able to unlock the back door without forcing my way in. The house was deserted. I went upstairs and found a bedroom with lots of warm bed covers on the bed, so I slept there on a warm bed for the first time in 8 months. I slept there more or less continually for 2 whole days and nights, I was so exhausted. However, I still had 2 massive problems: food and a bath or shower because I was filthy. I found that the water and electricity in the house had been cut off and there was no food. I went outside of the house in the middle of the night, so I couldn't be seen by MI5, to scout around for places to get food and a hot shower or a bath. I found other deserted places along the coast, both houses and restaurants, so I climbed through a window into another nearby, abandoned house to have a hot shower. The hot shower was beautiful, it was my first for approximately 9 months. Then I climbed into a restaurant through a window for food. I found a bag and filled it with food including a huge block of cheese, lots of bread and other food from the fridge, with which I could make a huge soup on the fire in my house. And this was how I lived from January to May 2005, in the winter in northern Greece, outside of Thessalonica. This was my worst ever time of having schizophrenia. My suffering was awful.

However, eventually, of course, in March 2005 the police came round to my house and took me away to the police station. They must have realized that I was just a starving, homeless tramp because they put me on a bus back to Thessalonika, and told me to go to the British Consulate there and go back to London. When I arrived at the British Consulate, they immediately phoned my mother in London for me, who transferred enough money to me for me to get a flight ticket back to London. I arrived back in London the next day and my mother met me at the airport. After I told her that I had the power of god, so MI5 were after me, and that Jackie Chan owed me 13 billion pounds for my Kung Fu, she called the mental health services, who came round, sectioned me for 3 months and took me away to the psychiatric ward at Saint Charles' hospital in Ladbroke Grove again.

"You've got Paranoid Schizophrenia"

Most mentally ill people are in denial when they're first admitted to a psychiatric ward. "There's nothing wrong with me and I'm being illegally detained" is exactly what they think and say, initially. Unfortunately, this isn't true. I was no different. I told a doctor that he wasn't really 'a doctor', he was just 'pretending to me to be a doctor' because he was really from 'MI5 to spy on me'. However, the doctors and social services are steadfast and adamant that if you don't take your medication and face up to your illness and delusions, you won't be leaving. So I eventually decided to take my medication again. There were a whole range of people on the ward, schizophrenics, manic depressives, and those who had drug and alcohol problems. However, the care and treatment on the NHS were really great. Patients had private rooms, 3 meals a day, and had to take medication every day. After my 3 month section was up, the doctors extended it for another 3 months, that's how chronically mentally ill I was. But I took my medication seriously in the end, attended all my weekly ward round meetings to talk to the doctors and social workers about my problems, and attended all the group therapy sessions that I could. Finally, in November 2005, my doctor, Dr. Evans, had called a private meeting with me. He said: 'you've got paranoid schizophrenia'. 'It's like this, if you take the medication, you can have a good life'. I decided, and agreed with him, then that I would take the medication every day for the rest of my life, to try and have the good life that he mentioned. Having demonstrated that I would always take my olanzapine pills every day, and having shown good behavior, I was discharged from hospital in December 2005, two weeks before Christmas.

However, being told that I had paranoid schizophrenia by the doctor was absolutely devastating for me. I realized that I was legally classed as mad, crazy and insane for the first time in all my experiences with it. I had to face up to the fact that I might be a lunatic or maniac or both. I really didn't know what I should make of it, how to take it or where my life should go from there. I wondered whether I was a lunatic or a maniac, and decided that I wasn't. I found it very, very depressing. I knew certainly that from then on, there was to be no more stopping taking the medication, for any reasons whatsoever. I simply had to make absolutely sure that I would take the medication for the rest of my life and not kid myself anymore, not delude myself, that is. I had always become ill when I had stopped taking the medication and the schizophrenia had come back and simply destroyed my life at those times.

I'd lost jobs, lost my daughter, lost earnings and lost beautiful women, who I wanted to get married to, and share my life with. I had a choice to make: take the medication and try to live as normal a life as possible or delude myself, go into denial about my psychological problems, and let the schizophrenia take over and perhaps destroy the whole of the rest of my life. I decided to stick with the medication because without it, I would spend the rest of my life suffering. I realized that the medication relieved my suffering. I didn't suffer from the chemical imbalances in the brain anymore, when I had taken my medication. And I didn't suffer from the mood swings anymore either, on the olanzapine. I didn't wake up anymore and suffer from the paranoia, depression or anger that I'd had, when my schizophrenia was full blown. My mum said it well for me: 'it must be a big relief being on the medication because you know you don't have to go through all that suffering anymore'.

Work, Career and Education

Once I was back home at my mum's, I started to look for a job again. And I managed to get a teaching job, teaching English and computers, at a central London adult, further education college. The job started in the new year in January 2006, so I had something positive to look forward to - a new routine working to get my normal life and self back together again. I was overjoyed to be working again. The students were really great. They were mostly asylum seekers from Africa but there were some European students in my classes too. All of my classes were elementary, basically for beginners, and I taught part time for 15 hours a week from the beginning of January to the end of June in 2006. I also got another job straight after that to teach foreign students in a summer school in central London, throughout July and August. All of the students were Europeans visiting London for the summer, and aiming to improve their English.

Working helped me tremendously to recover my mental health and it paid the bills for my flat and my general living expenses. I was comparatively lucky compared to most people with mental illnesses. Most of them that I was on the psychiatric ward with, claimed various, financial, welfare benefits from the government, whereas I chose to work, to try to have as normal a life as possible. Those who claimed benefits gave themselves little reason to live any more, as they stayed at home, unemployed all the time, and tended to compound their problems with drink or drugs. Their lives became meaningless. I've met schizophrenics who get discharged from hospital and then go and smoke marijuana all day to 'chill out'. Others get discharged from hospital and become alcoholics. I decided that wasn't for me. I had got myself a good education with my M.A degree, and decided I would try to work as much as possible, for as long as possible, for a meaningful life. I considered that working all the time would be as positive a life for me, as I could possibly get.

From the money I had saved up, I decided to do Cambridge university's CELTA course to update myself and my qualifications from October to November, which I did while taking time off work during those months. After my graduation with my CELTA certificate, I decided to look for jobs abroad, where the work was plentiful and where the teaching salaries were more than those in London. Also, I knew I could have a higher standard of living abroad than I could in London. I got lucky. I was offered a teaching job at the biggest and best language school in Hong Kong, which also ran Cambridge University's DELTA, teacher training course. I decided to take the job to start in January 2007 and, while teaching for the school, I also decided to study for the DELTA. I signed a 1 year contract with the school and started teaching there in January. I had chosen to teach only adults and my Chinese students were all very nice, polite and friendly people to me.

My life in teaching went well at the school in Hong Kong and I renewed my contract to stay with the school for a second year in 2008 to do the DELTA. I thought that doing the DELTA would make me the best teacher I could be, and would update my teaching skills and knowledge, so that I would always be able to get jobs in my future teaching career and so that I would be on an equal intellectual level with the best people in my profession. I also wanted to do the DELTA to prove to myself that I was completely mentally well again, and could mix it with the best. I started to read the 25 compulsory books for the DELTA course, 6 months before the course started in August 2007 for the start in February 2008. Then when the course started, I attended all of the compulsory input sessions, and did all the observed teaching practice. When I had completed those and the essay assignments, there was the exam, which I failed the first time in June 2008, and passed the second time with a re-take in December 2008. Finally, I received my DELTA from the University of Cambridge in March 2009. I felt I had made it back into the real world, I had done it, I had proved to myself that I was a contender in my profession and I was up there with the best. It was an outstanding success for me and a highlight of my life. I felt that I had fully recovered my mental faculties through studying.

After the course, I carried on teaching for the same school because I had been so successful with them. And I had decided to stay in Hong Kong with the school, because there was plenty of work with them and I had discovered that I could buy my anti-psychotic, medication olanzapine pills in Hong Kong, so I had a lifetime supply. This meant that I would never need to stop taking them again because they were so readily and easily available over the counter, possibly in any country in the world, because there are schizophrenia sufferers the world over, so I should never need to become ill again, because I would stay in Hong Kong for my pills and my work. I was with the same school for nearly 4 years from 2007 to 2010, without any recurrence of my schizophrenia, because I always took my pills every day to keep myself well. My teaching progressed well and I settled down into my life in Hong Kong, as one of the best qualified teachers there. I met my Chinese fiancé 'My' there, who wanted to have children with me and settle down.

The Present day

My paranoid schizophrenia has always led to me being more of a danger to myself than to others. It has always started off with me becoming extremely religious, whereas in my real, sane life I am a devout atheist. This is how my schizophrenia has previously deceived my own mind. It starts with voices, which convince the sufferer that God is talking to them. Then there are hallucinations of God, angels or spirits, so the sufferer believes he is having a supernatural, psychic experience. And then come the paranoid delusions and grandiosity, based on the voices and hallucinations. By this time, of course, the sufferer is totally deluded. After, or during, the schizophrenic voices and hallucinations, I have started going to church and brainwashing myself with the Bible because I have believed I'm hearing voices from God. My hallucinations and voices from heaven have seemed so real to me that I have gone off on religious pilgrimages with little or no money to support myself, so I have always ended up a filthy, homeless tramp on a top secret, holy mission from God.

This has always been the great, grandiose delusion: that somehow I'm Jesus in the second coming, coming to perform miracles with the power of God, and coming to judge the world. This is why I've had the paranoia of the CIA, FBI, KGB and MI5 being after me – because I have the power of God. Once I've become a homeless, starving, filthy tramp, the schizophrenia has deluded my mind that I'm really on a holy pilgrimage as Jesus was. I was on the verge of freezing and starving to death in the night in the freezing cold mountains of Greece but I kept on riding my bike to stay alive because the voices deluded me into thinking I was on a holy pilgrimage. I kept on rummaging through dustbins for food in Thessalonika for 7 months because the voices deluded me into thinking that this is what Jesus should do – live without money. Eventually, I have always had to end up at a British Consulate in Barcelona, Bangkok or Athens, so they could phone my mum for a ticket home and so that I could go back to taking my medication on a psychiatric ward in a mental hospital. The paranoid schizophrenia has made me walk away from good jobs in Istanbul, London and Jakarta to become a homeless tramp on an imaginary, holy pilgrimage. That's how much it has damaged me and disrupted my teaching career and, therefore, my life. All of this has, potentially, been very dangerous for me because I could have been attacked at any time, when I was a tramp living on the streets or rummaging through dustbins for food. I could have been killed on the dangerous roads of Greece, while I was riding a mountain bike for months visiting churches. I was a danger to myself. I am very grateful to all of the mental health services and psychiatrists who have treated me during my suffering and who have, therefore, saved my life.

I had started out becoming interested in, and converting to, Buddhism, when I lived in Thailand with my wife, in my twenties. Then I had progressed onto Christianity, going to church, taking Bible study classes and studying it in my spare time. Then my schizophrenia developed and my delusions were all religious, based on all the religious books I'd ever read. Originally, I thought that my search for the truth of life necessarily involved studying the major religions and religious books. Now I realize that I had been gravely mistaken. My beliefs in religion and spirituality were the route in which my schizophrenia had always deceived my own mind. It had all been bad for my mental health.

I heard recently in the media about Anders Bhering Breivik in Norway, who detonated a bomb there, and then went on to murder a certain number of youths, who were at a youth camp in Norway. According to reports, when psychiatrists assessed him they found that he was suffering from delusions that Muslims were taking over Europe, and so he blamed the Norwegian government and committed horrendous acts of violence on innocent people because of his delusions. It was my opinion then, when I heard that, that he was suffering from paranoid schizophrenic delusions. Obviously, he needed treatment for his illness and to be on medication for the long term. This would, arguably, have relieved him of suffering from his delusions and, hopefully, would have saved lives. He was obviously a danger to others. That said, some sources report that only approximately 5% of violent crime is committed by people with mental health problems. I had been very lucky to have established a good teaching career for myself.

A few years ago I saw a film called, 'The Exorcism of Emily Rose'. It was based on a real life case of exorcism, which was carried out in the 1970s on a girl named Anneliese Michel. There were two differing positions in the film. They revolved around a court case, in which the prosecution believed that the girl was physically, and possibly mentally, ill and the defense believed that she had suffered from demon possession. The girl had died and the prosecution blamed the family priest for letting the girl come off her medication and performing an exorcism. With my knowledge of the voices, hallucinations and delusions of schizophrenia, I would like to state that, when I saw the film, I believed that the girl was suffering from all of the symptoms of schizophrenia that I have suffered from, and not from demon possession as claimed by the priest in the film. According to the film, she heard religious voices, had hallucinations of demons and holy Mary and believed she was possessed, as her family did too. These are some of the symptoms of my schizophrenia, which I believe this girl also suffered from, after my seeing the film. I do not believe she suffered from possession but, rather, mental illness. Paranoid persecutory delusions are symptoms of paranoid schizophrenia, a chemical imbalance in the brain, and they are relieved by being treated with anti psychotic medication, not by exorcism.

In history, particularly in the Bible, people believed that there was such a thing as being possessed by the devil or demons. This appears to have been the overwhelming, historical, religious perspective. Consequently, exorcisms were performed by priests or Jesus' disciples who engaged in the placing on of hands or the chanting of religious prayers for those 'possessed'. However, due to the rapid advances of medical science in modern times, we now know that medicine can treat mental illness, which people in previous centuries didn't know. Medical science was simply not available to the mentally ill in the past, so religious priests were thought to have all the answers and the cure to the problem. Thanks to modern psychiatry, we now know that they were wrong.

After studying science to educate myself, I now believe that Charles Darwin's evolution disproves the creations in the Bible, Koran and in the Torah. Therefore, in my opinion, these religious books and beliefs are not true, and are no longer part of my beliefs about life and the world. In many previous centuries in history, science hadn't developed enough, or wasn't studied enough, to prove religion wrong, now it is. The religions, arguably, appear to be made up of myths and legends that people wrote down in religious texts and attributed to God, because they weren't educated enough, or hadn't developed science enough, to explain the world with the scientific facts, which we can today. Modern scientific facts about life and the world simply weren't available to people in the past to explain the world, as they are today. So people invented religions and wrote religious books in their first primitive attempts to explain things to themselves and each other. In my opinion, no one has ever been able to prove creation, spirits, angels, demons or a devil. Science has, in my opinion, now filled this gap in people's knowledge, if they choose to accept it. It's my personal belief that the holocaust of the Jewish people during world war two disproves all the Gods of the world's major religions completely. In the same way, I believe that the colonial, African slave trade does too.

Conclusion

It's now 2012 and I'm busy with my working life. On a usual working day, I wake up at 6 o'clock in the morning, and make some coffee for myself, which I have with two or three cigarettes. This usually takes about half an hour. Then I'm ready for a shower. After my shower, I get dressed for my university where I'm teaching, and walk to my local bus stop to get the 7 o'clock bus to work. The bus takes about 35 minutes to arrive at my university. Once I arrive, I go to my office to check emails and work directives on my computer. I'm in my university classroom ready to teach at 8 o'clock. I usually like to start by warming my class up with a friendly chat about their everyday lives, how they're getting on at home and how their studies are going. I have, on average, about 20 students in each of my classes. They're between the ages of 18 and 21 and they're all studying English for their government, university, educational requirements and for their future careers. After the chat and taking the register, I write up the lesson on the board including, of, course, the language that they're going to study today. Then they start practicing in pairs and groups.

The lesson ends at 10 o'clock and it's time for my breakfast. I'll have some tea and scrambled eggs on toast at a local café, and then some coffee and a few cigarettes with my colleagues outside after that. Then I'll go for a walk around the streets nearby to do some window shopping or I'll sit outside another local café and have some more coffee with my colleagues and chat. After this, it's time for me to read a newspaper online back in my office, to catch up with what's going on in the world. Then I plan and prepare for my afternoon classes, which start at 1 o'clock. My afternoon classes are usually more relaxed than my morning ones. This is because we have already done a major amount of work in the morning, so the afternoons are usually just focused on speaking practice or writing. My students will often just want to chat to me about what life is like in the English speaking western countries, how it's different from their countries or about the other academic, university subjects that they are studying on their university timetables. Some students want to spend the whole lesson talking to me about my life, their lives, or my opinions about any given topics that they bring up from the latest world or local news, which they have an interest in. Then we might all have a big, interesting discussion together as a class. The class ends at 3 o'clock and then I'll take the bus home again. When I get home, I might take my nightly medication early at about 6 or 7 pm, or I might take it later at about 9 pm, just before I go to bed.

I spend my spare time and my weekends reading books and newspapers, watching the news on television and going to pubs and bars to watch premier league football with friends. I've always been a big football fan, so I make sure I keep up to date with my team's progress. I've been taking my medication solidly for 7 years now and in that time I haven't had any recurrence of my symptoms. I'm keeping myself well. I have been very lucky with my life, because I've got myself a good education and a steady career to keep myself busy, and to earn good money to live on. I visit my local doctor once every 6 weeks to get new prescriptions for my medication, which I take daily. I see my daughter regularly in my spare time. She likes me to take her out to eat at restaurants and to the cinema. She's in her final year of university and she hopes to graduate with her Bachelor degree next year.

Lightning Source UK Ltd.
Milton Keynes UK
UKOW04f1044260713

214365UK00001B/23/P